the Doctrine
of Adoption?

Basics of the Faith

Sean Michael Lucas, Series Editor

What Is the Doctrine of Adoption?

Michael A. Milton

P&R
PUBLISHING

P.O. BOX 817 • PHILLIPSBURG • NEW JERSEY 08865-0817

Unless otherwise indicated, Scripture quotations are from *ESV Bible* ® (*The Holy Bible, English Standard Version* ®). Copyright © 2001 by Crossway Bibles, a publishing ministry of Good News Publishers. Used by permission. All rights reserved.

Italics within Scripture quotations indicate emphasis added.

Page design by Tobias Design

Printed in the United States of America

Library of Congress Cataloging-in-Publication Data

Milton, Michael A. (Michael Anthony), 1958-
 What is the doctrine of adoption? / Michael A. Milton.
     p. cm. -- (Basics of the faith)
 Includes bibliographical references and index.
 ISBN 978-1-59638-391-3 (pbk.)
 1. Adoption (Theology) I. Title.
  BT165.M55 2012
  234--dc23

                        2011042958

ADOPTION IS SO MUCH MORE

The Westminster Shorter Catechism defines the doctrine of adoption this way:

> Adoption is an act of God's free grace, whereby we are received into the number, and have a right to all the privileges of the sons of God. (Shorter Catechism, Question 34)[1]

Yet the doctrine of adoption, described with brevity and clarity in this catechism, is worthy of a deeper study. This glorious and most beautiful truth of God's Word is too often overlooked, under-taught or rendered indistinguishable from other doctrines, such as justification and sanctification, in the order of salvation. This is what theologian Professor John Murray (1898–1975) meant when he wrote the following:

> Adoption is an act of God's grace distinct from and additional to the other acts of grace involved in the application of redemption. It might seem unnecessary to say this. . . . Too frequently it has been regarded as simply an aspect of justification or as

another way of stating the privilege conferred by regeneration. It is much more than either or both of these acts of grace.[2]

I have seen Murray's opinion fleshed out in countless counseling sessions with those professing faith in Christ. A continued lack of understanding of this key doctrine can lead to mental confusion, lack of assurance, spiritual depression, and various other diseases of the soul. The cause of this misunderstanding comes from a combination of several dark sources: a lack of knowledge of the whole counsel of God, satanic attack, lies to self or others, doctrinal distortions, misunderstandings, and blatant false teachings of this "present evil age."[3]

Why is it worth our while to consider the doctrine of adoption? In a word, freedom: "And you will know the truth, and the truth will set you free" (John 8:32). As it is revealed in God's Word, adoption remains, from beginning to end, a unique and necessary truth to be received, taught, and embraced personally by believers and corporately by church congregations. A correct understanding produces a healthy, balanced view of God, others, and self. As Dr. Joel Beeke has written,

> Adoption is heavenly before it is earthly. One is what God does; the other is what we do. Adoption is something God has done and is doing before it is something we have done and are doing. God invented adoption even before He created the world. Adoption is how God brings us into His family.[4]

It is my prayer that this little book in the Basics of the Faith series by P&R Publishing will bring about God's own intention: that those who trust in Jesus Christ as the resurrected and living Lord should no longer live as "cosmic orphans," alone in a cold, postmodern age of nonabsolutes. Instead, they should live as sons and daughters of the living God, secure forever in the growing family of a loving heavenly Father who will never let us go.

THE DOCTRINE OF ADOPTION IN LIFE

Adoption is not a process. Adoption is not an identity. Adoption is a singular, nonrepeatable, unilateral event based on love, choice, sacrifice, and law, which binds the parties forever by an authoritative decree. I know that. I was not "given up"; I was *placed*. I was placed to become a son with a home and a name and a new life. I am not an "adopted person." Rather, I *was* adopted.

The question of what language to use for adoption—in the earthly or the heavenly family—is not just a matter of sensitivities and politeness. In the New Testament the Greek word for adoption is a "presumed" compound of the Greek word *huios*, "son," and the word *titheœmi*, "to place." Adoption is therefore, according to the Greek word employed by the Holy Spirit, most properly, "the placing of a son, or child, into a welcoming family." This also shows dignity as we contemplate all sides of adoption, including the human realm for the birth parent (or the court, as in my own case) who must make a plan to "place"—not give up—the child.

My father's sister, my Aunt Eva, adopted me when I was orphaned as a young child. The proposal came before a judge, and he made his authoritative ruling and placed me in the arms of Aunt Eva legally, just as I had been physically placed in her arms before that. By the judge's word the law of the land was applied to the love and choice of my aunt, and in one decree, one moment, from the ashes of my story and the desire and prayers of my Aunt Eva's story—a childless 65-year-old widow—a new story began: our story together. Once the story was settled, she never referred to me as her "adopted son." Sometimes I hear others refer to their children this way. Insensitive and thoughtless remarks about "real children" versus "adopted children" make adoption an ongoing identity rather than a once-and-forever event. They elevate bloodline over covenant, a wrongheaded, human way of thinking in fleshly juxtaposition to the concept of family presented in the Bible.[5]

Unchecked and unexplained, this misguided talk about adoption can ultimately lead to the appearance of malignancies of the human soul, mental anguish, a crisis of personhood, and a host of other diseases of the heart and mind. This is true for both the child and the parent. Just ask a parent whose child was born to them through adoption whether they have heard hurtful remarks; you will hear stories with anger and with tears.[6] I heard others whisper about the widow woman who adopted a little baby as we were in the market, the hardware store, and other places around town. But I thank God that Aunt Eva never used the word "adopted" when she spoke to others about me. I was just her boy, her son, her child just like any other child placed by God into this or that family. Her wording was indicative of more than just wise insight into the heart of her child. It was legal language and, as we shall see, her attitude and actions concerning adoption were radically biblical.

Justin Taylor wrote on his experiences as a father of a child "born" to them through adoption. In dealing with insensitive questions like "Is that your real child?" he wrote these words: "But sometimes I wonder if the way we speak about physical, earthly adoption shows that we have not yet let the truths about spiritual adoption truly sink into our hearts and minds."[7]

In fact, my Aunt Eva believed in the truths about "spiritual adoption." She reared me as her son, loved me as her son, wept over me when I was her prodigal son, and prayed for her son to return to God. The day finally came when she saw the answer to her prayer and rejoiced over her saved son.

As Aunt Eva grew older, my wife Mae and I took care of her. She was my mother and that was right. When our son was born, through adoption, she rejoiced at her grandchild. At almost 99 years of age, when she knew the Lord was calling her home, she raised her hands and blessed my wife and son. She pulled me down to her and whispered in my ear, "Son, keep up the good work of the Lord."

Had she been a rich woman I would have received more than the tattered old family Bible, a shoebox full of fading black and white photos (of mostly unidentified people who had once meant something to her), and a few household remnants that she kept. That is all she had. It was so little, but I did inherit what she had left. It was only right. I was her heir. I was her son.

Although this book is not about family adoption, we cannot answer the question "What is the doctrine of adoption?" without referring to families. Family adoption has its reference in God's love and free choice of us as His sons and daughters. God's adoption of us as His sons and daughters helps us understand adoption in family life.

R. E. Ciampa, in his article on adoption in the *New Dictionary of Biblical Theology*, defines adoption as "the legal establishment of a kinship relationship between two people that is recognized as being equivalent to one based on physical descent."[8] We need that good, sturdy, concise definition.

We need to know that family relations are more than DNA and bloodlines according to the Bible.[9]

One example of the Bible's definition of families is that relationships are formed in Leviticus according to marriage, not bloodline alone—with the effect of restricting who may be married to each other. For instance, a father's son may not marry his deceased father's wife. This understanding, known as consanguinity and affinity, refers thus to blood and affinity through marriage. See Leviticus 18:6–23 and 20:11–21. See also the case studies of Herod's relationship with his brother Philip's wife in Matthew 14:3–4 and of Paul's condemnation of a son marrying his father's wife in 1 Corinthians 5:1.

As with family adoptions, when biblical adoption is not understood or believed, the same hurtful questions emerge.

- Are you *really* God's son, given where you came from and what you have done?
- Are you *really* brothers and sisters since you come from such different backgrounds?
- Will you *really* be loved and welcomed into God's family with the baggage that you bring with you?
- I wonder if adoption means that I will *always* be God's daughter? What if I do something bad? Can this be *reversed*? *Will He always be my Father?*
- Does adoption make me different from others? Is this special identity good or peculiar?
- The world says that adoption is a second choice, leads to questions of identity, and seeks to perpetuate a story of an inner wound in search of a healing.[10] Is that my destiny as God's child? Am I destined to spend my life seeking my *real* identity?
- Am I whole? Can I ever feel complete?

These existential questions are important. They are important because you or many of those around you are asking them. And there are answers. Some of those answers originate from the philosophies of man or even the diabolical suggestions of mankind's enemy. The world and the devil fill us with so many wrongheaded notions about "flesh versus covenant relations," and hurt, pain, and confusion fester from such ideas.

As a pastor and a minister of the gospel serving a seminary, I long to explain the scriptural doctrine of adoption. I believe that the apostle Paul had that longing too. Have you noticed that nothing changes? There is nothing new under the sun. The same bad teaching or absent teaching on adoption has always been present, with the same tragic results. This is why Paul wrote to believers in his day because he did not want the flock of Jesus, the daughters and sons of God, limping through life as spiritual orphans. So he would teach, with warmhearted pastoral sensitivity,

> So you are no longer a slave, but a son, and if a son, then an heir through God (Gal. 4:7).

> So then you are no longer strangers and aliens, but you are fellow citizens with the saints and members of the household of God (Eph. 2:19).

As we transition from thinking about the relationship of family adoption to spiritual adoption, we would do well to meditate on the words of the good old Puritan Thomas Watson. He helps us see that, as wonderful as physical adoption is, like all attempts at trying to describe what God does for us in Christ in human similes and comparisons, we cannot completely describe the ethereal, unsearchable glory of God's goodness. We are left to praise Him without fully comprehending the unfathomable richness and insuperable love of our Savior in adoption.

> Extol and magnify God's mercy, who has adopted you into his family; who, of slaves, has made you sons; of heirs of hell, heirs of the promise. Adoption is a free gift. He gave them power, or dignity, to become the sons of God. As a thread of silver runs through a whole piece of work, so free grace runs through the whole privilege of adoption. Adoption is greater mercy than Adam had in paradise; he was a son by creation, but here is a further sonship by adoption. To make us thankful, consider, in civil adoption there is some worth and excellence in the person to be adopted; but there was no worth in us, neither beauty, nor parentage, nor virtue; nothing in us to move God to bestow the prerogative of sonship upon us. We have enough in us to move God to correct us, but nothing to move him to adopt us, therefore exalt free grace; begin the work of angels here; bless him with your praises who has blessed you in making you his sons and daughters.[11]

As we move forward in this little book, which I prefer to be a pastoral epistle to your heart from the Word of God, here is my sincere prayer for you:

> Let the truth of the doctrine of adoption shine through, O Christ, that Your people—this person reading this book—may be free, that we may be the happy and secure children that You have called us to be. Let this little book be used of Your Spirit, O God, in some way, to

magnify the steadfast love of You, O Father, to little
boys and girls who desperately need to know that we
have a family; to know who we are in Christ Jesus. I
ask this in Jesus' name. Amen!

Let's get going.[12]

SCRIPTURAL TEACHING ON THE DOCTRINE OF ADOPTION

The Old Testament, as well as the New Testament, teaches
the doctrine of adoption. It is clearly taught as revealed doctrine in the New Testament passages that we shall examine,
and it is taught in sacred story and divine example in the
Old Testament, while admittedly in its primordial form. The
Bible, when studied as a whole, teaches us that the doctrine
of adoption is related to the revelation of four ways in which
the almighty God expresses fatherhood.

Before we move forward, it is good at this point to take
a more systematic-theological overview of God's fatherhood
in the Bible. God's fatherhood is, first, to quote Murray—as
I shall do in all but one of the names for God's fatherhood—
intertrinitarian. We cannot relate to God's fatherhood in
this revealed way. We will never be sons in the same way
Jesus is a Son. There are Scriptures that speak of the love
of Father God for His Son within the Trinity. An example of
this is in the intimate language that the Son uses in John 10,
verses 18 and 29 respectively: "No one takes it from me, but I
lay it down of my own accord. I have authority to lay it down,
and I have authority to take it up again. This charge I have
received from my Father"; "My Father, who has given them
to me, is greater than all, and no one is able to snatch them
out of the Father's hand."

The Scriptures also teach about God's creative fatherhood. God is the Father of all men according to Paul in his
sermon on Mars Hill:

For

" 'In him we live and move and have our being';

as even some of your own poets have said,

" 'For we are indeed his offspring.'

Being then God's offspring, we ought not to think
that the divine being is like gold or silver or stone,
an image formed by the art and imagination of man."
(Acts 17:28–29)

The third model of adoption in the Bible is theocratic.
This is God's fatherhood related to Israel, as when God
instructed Moses: "Then you shall say to Pharaoh, 'Thus
says the LORD, Israel is my firstborn son' " (Ex. 4:22).

Finally, there is the New Testament reality of adoption that John Murray calls adoptive fatherhood, but that I
prefer to call New Testament or new covenant fatherhood.
This does not mean that it differs from the way God adopted
saints into His family in the Old Testament, but because of
the full dispensation of redemption through Jesus Christ,
we see that the doctrine comes alive explicitly in this new
dispensation. In Galatians 3:23–4:6, the apostle Paul unites
theocratic fatherhood and new covenant fatherhood per-
fectly. Two key passages form the chain between the Old
and New: "And if you are Christ's, then you are Abraham's
offspring, heirs according to promise" (Gal. 3:29); and this

typically dramatic, doxological climax to the progression of thought,

> But when the fullness of time had come, God sent forth his Son, born of woman, born under the law, to redeem those who were under the law, so that we might receive adoption as sons. And because you are sons, God has sent the Spirit of his Son into our hearts, crying, "Abba Father!" (Gal. 4:4–6)

These four models of God's fatherhood help us to understand His love for His Son Jesus and His love for His own creation (yet the doctrine of adoption denies that all men are adopted), and then for you, His child that He redeemed through His Son Jesus and calls His own. The language of love, the language of family, the example of a spiritual adoption is present in each.

Old Testament Teaching on Adoption

The New Testament affirms the doctrine of adoption in the Old Testament: "They are Israelites, and to them belong the *adoption*, the glory, the covenants, the giving of the law, the worship, and the promises" (Rom. 9:4). An in-depth study of the Old Testament prototype of New Testament "new covenant adoption" begins with God and His relationship to Israel, as well as to those who were Gentiles and grafted into God's family. John Murray in his eminent study of the doctrine of adoption in his book, *Redemption Accomplished and Applied*, identifies key texts for grasping the doctrine in the Old Testament.[13] I will give brief comments on the texts, but first I would like to add two narratives that point to the doctrine of adoption. In fact, I find these more potent and more easily understandable. These include the adoption of Rahab into the family of Israel, and the adoption of Ruth into the old covenant family. Both of these women are listed in the genealogy of our Lord Jesus Christ in Matthew 1:5.

The story of Rahab is the story of a woman in Jericho, not just any woman but a prostitute who chose to cast her lot with Israel. Joshua, representing the people of God, saved Rahab and her father's household and all who belonged to her, and she came into Israel. She was, in every sense, adopted into the people of God. The writer to the Hebrews lists her as a heroine of the faith when he recorded the following: "By faith Rahab the prostitute did not perish with those who were disobedient, because she had given a friendly welcome to the spies" (Heb. 11:31).

Rehab's faith—a rejection of her former life and her own sinful people and a trust in the God of Israel—led her to be redeemed, and that regeneration of her life led to her adoption. "But Rahab the prostitute and her father's household and all who belonged to her, Joshua saved alive. And she has lived in Israel to this day, because she hid the messengers whom Joshua sent to spy out Jericho" (Josh. 6:25). This woman of God, formerly a Gentile and a vile sinner, became a grandmother of our Savior. Rahab was adopted into the family of God.

Ruth's story is located in a book of the Bible that bears her name. Ruth was a Moabite, another Gentile woman. She had married a Hebrew man from Bethlehem who had sojourned to her country during a time of famine in Israel. This Hebrew man died, as did his father and his brother. His mother, Naomi, heard that the famine was over, prepared to go back to Israel, and urged her daughters-in-law to return to their own land. Orpah did return to Moab, but Ruth did not. Something had happened in her heart and life that was deeper than her love of her country and her old life. We read these remarkable words:

> And she said, "See, your sister-in-law has gone back to her people and to her gods; return after your sister-in-

law." But Ruth said, "Do not urge me to leave you or to return from following you. For where you go I will go, and where you lodge I will lodge. Your people shall be my people, and your God my God." (Ruth 1:15–16)

Once again, we encounter an Old Testament narrative in which a Gentile woman repudiates her old life and identifies herself with God. This repentance and faith lead to adoption. It is important not to confuse the sequence of doctrinal stakes that are placed by the Holy Spirit in this historical account. There was a witness of true faith in the one true God by Naomi (and presumably, if not demonstrably, by her late husband), there was renunciation of the past life of Moabite gods and the people who followed them, and there was a commitment of faith to the Lord. The story then moves to God's provision for this childless woman by giving her a "redeemer" from the family. Boaz, this godly man, takes her as his wife. The Lord blesses the couple with a child, Obed. The sweet story concludes in perfect literary resolution with the child in the lap of Naomi, his surrogate grandmother. The final verses, a genealogy, are not to be overlooked:

Salmon fathered Boaz, Boaz fathered Obed, Obed fathered Jesse, and Jesse fathered David. (Ruth 4:21–22)

Again in Matthew 1 Ruth is listed as Jesus' forebearer through the adoptive line of Joseph.[14] Thus, Ruth was adopted into the family of God.

The doctrine of adoption is introduced in Old Testament narrative even as it is more explicitly revealed in Old Testament relationship between God and His covenanted people. Let us turn our attention to other Old Testament texts that help us, from a theocratic fatherhood view of God, to see the doctrine of adoption. We will consider two of the many Old Testament passages available for study.

"For you are a people holy to the LORD your God, and the LORD has chosen you to be a people for his treasured possession, out of all the peoples who are on the face of the earth" (Deut. 14:2). It is important to see that this passage, which is essential to understanding the relationship of the ancient church (Israel) to God, is grounded in God's adoption of Israel. We would do well to note that is the exact case in the New Testament passages. The children of God are just so because God chose them, they are treasured, they are His possession; they are to be differentiated from all the other peoples of the earth.

It is critical to note that while God is in a real sense the father of all creation (Acts 17:26–28), He is not the father of all in the same way He is to those He has adopted as His own children. One may think of a teacher who calls her class "my children," for she nurtures them, instructs them, and is responsible for them. Yet those children are to be differentiated from children in her family. The most devoted teacher would not say that her classroom children are her "treasure" in the same way the children of her household and family are. God is the father of mankind, but God is the father of His own household, His own intimate family. Israel, that is the family of Abraham, Isaac, and Jacob (Israel), became the children of God from among all the nations because of His sovereign grace. Moses reminded the Hebrew children that they were chosen by God not because they were greater in number or more righteous than any other nation, but only because of God's sovereign choice (Deut. 4:37; 7:7; 9:4; 10:15).[15]

The prophet Isaiah mentions Abraham and Jacob (Israel) since it was through those two, more so than Isaac, that the covenant was clearly ratified. "For you are our Father, though Abraham does not know us, and Israel does not acknowledge us; you, O LORD, are our Father, our Redeemer from of old is your name" (Isa. 63:16). Yet the relationship of the Hebrews did not depend on those men, but on their true Father, the Lord.

John Calvin believed that this passage was, indeed, an Old Testament example of the doctrine of adoption. He wrote the following in his commentary on Isaiah:

> Redemption is here described as a testimony of that adoption; for by this proof God manifested himself to be the Father of the people; and therefore boldly and confidently do believers call on God as their Father, because he gave a remarkable testimony of his fatherly kindness toward them, which encouraged them to confidence.[16]

And the doctrine of adoption could not be more clearly taught by Calvin than when he preached from this Old Testament passage:

> Sooner shall the rights of nature perish than thou shalt not act toward us as a Father, or the sacred adoption shall be infringed, which was founded on Thy unchangeable decree, and ratified by the death of Thine only-begotten Son.[17]

My heart is moved to prayer and praise even as I contemplate this passage now! I write to you with this passage exploding into my own heart with joy and thanksgiving to Jesus Christ my Lord! This is what the truth of adoption in Christ does for us, my dear reader. Oh that this moment, in the midst of this little book, you will put down your arguments with God, lay your sincerest existential interrogations of the pain in your life at the foot of the cross of Calvary, and fly to the Savior! Go not to Calvin, Luther, or Wesley for that matter; nor rely on a blood relationship with Moses or Abraham—they are guides that each went to the One you now seek—but go to the author and finisher of our salvation.[18] Come and know your Father. Come and know that you are a child of the living God. Heaven and earth will pass away, but God's love for you, whom He has redeemed through His blessed Son Jesus Christ, and justified by His unalterable decree, shall never pass away. You are a son; you are a daughter, forever!

Let us turn to the new covenant fatherhood of God examples in the New Testament.

New Testament Teaching on Adoption

The New Testament, like the Old, continues to teach us through case studies within narratives—story—as well as through explicit doctrinal instruction. One could reach deeply into the narratives in the Gospels, or in Dr. Luke's chronicle of the early church, and find repeated cases of Gentiles and vile sinners who were gloriously regenerated and adopted into the family of God through the ministry of our Lord Jesus or of His apostles. Human lives and even cultures were changed, and history—theirs and ours—was reshaped by their new familial relationship with God. I shall pass over many to bring you three.

The Case of the Roman Centurion. In the case of the Roman centurion in Matthew 8 and Luke 7, we see a military man representing a most vicious oppressor of Israel. He had a servant who was both paralyzed and suffering greatly.[19] He came to Jesus, calling Him "Lord," and appealed to Christ for his servant. Jesus agreed to go to his home. Yet this Roman officer replied in words that have come down through history to us today, remembered in our Communion liturgies—the very language of our family meal. Many Christians all over the world repeat his words each week at Communion in the Prayer of Humble Access: "Lord, I am not worthy to have you come under my roof, but only say the word, and my servant will be healed" (Matt. 8:8).[20]

Jesus declared that this Gentile soldier had greater faith than any in Israel (which included His disciples!).[21] This Roman centurion's faith not only brought a miracle to his servant but also justified him before God as he trusted in Christ. He was adopted to become a child of our heavenly Father.

The Case of Lydia. Then there is the remarkable case of Lydia, the first convert in Europe.[22] The great Charles Haddon Spurgeon, in a sermon he called "Lydia, the First European Convert," began his sermon by observing how God founded Western Christianity on the faith of this woman, not a preacher or a great nobleman but a woman: "I half envy Lydia that she should be the leader of the European band; yet I feel right glad that a woman led the van, and that her household followed so closely in the rear."[23] We see a remarkable woman who repented and believed. She and her husband helped advance the gospel in the West. She was adopted to become a child of our heavenly Father.

The Case of the Philippian Jailer. The Philippian jailer, a pagan serving the cause of the enemies of God, was regenerated after seeing the power of God at work in the life of his prisoner, Paul.

> Then he brought them out and said, "Sirs, what must I do to be saved?" And they said, "Believe in the Lord Jesus, and you will be saved, you and your household." And they spoke the word of the Lord to him and to all who were in his house. And he took them the same hour of the night and washed their wounds; and he

was baptized at once, he and all his family. Then he brought them up into his house and set food before them. And he rejoiced along with his entire household that he had believed in God (Acts 16:30–34).

Once again we may trace the divine pattern of regeneration, justification, and adoption. The baptism by Paul marked the sign to this Philippian jailer and to his whole household of the new covenant life that follows faith. This man was adopted to become a child of our heavenly Father.

The Case of Our Lord Himself. The second person of the Trinity was never adopted by God to be His Son. That is a heresy condemned by the early church and disproved by many Scriptures.[24] Yet we may look to our Lord in His earthly life and learn something of the doctrine of adoption. The greatest example of adoption in the whole Bible and in human history is the adoption of Jesus, the only begotten Son of God, to become the earthly son of Joseph. Joseph gave Jesus His name. Jesus' lineage is traced through this man of God.

> And Jacob the father of Joseph the husband of Mary, of whom Jesus was born, who is called Christ. (Matt. 1:16)

> Jesus, when he began his ministry, was about thirty years of age, being the son (as was supposed) of Joseph, the son of Heli. (Luke 3:23)

Joseph protected Jesus from the brutal hand of Herod. Joseph gave our Savior His earthy vocation as a carpenter. Our Savior was and is the Son of God, the second person of the Trinity. Yet He was and always remains now God in the flesh, the Son of God and of the Virgin Mary. Yet Joseph adopted Jesus as his son and Jesus obeyed His earthly father and honored him as such. How sweet and lovely is this truth when we consider the teaching of our spiritual adoption. God knows all about adoption.

We can see that each of these narrative accounts holds a storehouse of rich, encouraging, and faith-building biblical nutrients for the believer to ingest. There are more. However, my allotted space in this pastoral epistle is limited (and I hope its brevity will encourage you to read it through and do greater study on this important, life-transforming truth), so I must focus on some principal passages from the New Testament on the doctrine of adoption.

Key Explicit New Testament Texts on the Doctrine of Adoption

The new covenant fatherhood of God brings astounding blessings to us through the truth that sets us free about our identity in Christ. We believers are given the deep, soul-satisfying news that our heavenly Father has accepted us as sons. The doctrine of adoption in the New Testament gives four affirmations in the extraordinary key passages that follow. As a theologian, I would recommend studying the whole as well as the parts of each passage. As a pastor, I would recommend saying the Scripture out loud and repeating the expository affirmation.

> For you did not receive the spirit of slavery to fall back into fear, but you have received the Spirit of adoption as sons, by whom we cry, "Abba Father!" (Rom. 8:15)

Affirmation Number One: The doctrine of adoption explains how God has redeemed me from the forces of fear that would keep me from claiming my identity as a son or daughter of the Lord, and it lifts me out of the pain of my orphan past into the pleasures of family life with our loving Father.

> And not only the creation, but we ourselves, who have the firstfruits of the Spirit, groan inwardly as we wait eagerly for adoption as sons, the redemption of our bodies. (Rom. 8:23)

I love the way George Whitefield put it:

> First we are in bondage, afterwards we receive the Spirit of adoption to long and thirst for God because He has been pleased to let us know that He will take us to heaven.[25]

Affirmation Number Two: The doctrine of adoption confirms the longing that I have within my heart—a longing born out of the ministry of the Holy Spirit at work within me for face-to-face intimacy with my Creator, and a longing to be with Him, body and soul, forever and ever.

> But when the fullness of time had come, God sent forth his Son, born of woman, born under the law, to redeem those who were under the law, so that we might receive adoption as sons. And because you are sons, God has sent the Spirit of his Son into our hearts, crying, "Abba Father!" (Gal. 4:4–6)

Affirmation Number Three: The doctrine of adoption teaches me that my relationship to the Father as His son or daughter is based solely on the redemptive act of the only begotten Son of God, Jesus Christ. It is never my own doing, for I am unable to make myself a son to anyone, and my sonship is sealed by the Holy Spirit who speaks through me, crying "Abba! Father!", my ransomed soul's innermost shout of joy. "In love he predestined us for adoption as sons through Jesus Christ, according to the purpose of his will" (Eph. 1:4–5).

Affirmation Number Four: The doctrine of adoption assures me that my sonship, brought about through the life obedience and blood atonement on the cross of my Lord Jesus Christ, was secured by an unchangeable decree of God in a great eternity past. I am born again as His child because of my Father's unsearchable, profound, yet fully expressed love for me.

It is my prayer that the doctrine of adoption will now move from text to soul and bring the assurance of your identity in Christ that God desires to give you.

OTHER REFLECTIONS ON THE DOCTRINE OF ADOPTION

To better grasp the rich meaning and applications of the doctrine of adoption, we can now stand on the shoulders of giants who have gone before us and soak in their succinct reflections of the same Scriptures on adoption we just encountered. We can also listen to the voices from our own day.

Reflections from the Westminster Confession of Faith (1646)

The English-speaking Puritans included something in their confessional statement that no other confessional had until that time. The Westminster divines (pastors) devoted an entire chapter to the subject of the doctrine of adoption.[26] Chapter twelve of the Westminster Confession of Faith, along with question 74 in the Westminster Larger Catechism and question 34 in the Shorter Catechism, all draw the believer to this essential truth of the gospel. Why? The Puritans were extraordinarily experiential in their theology. You might say that they wanted to "put legs on their theology." Adoption does that. The doctrine in the Word of God that follows regeneration and justification needed to have a place then as now *because the body of Christ in all ages needs the assurance that we are sons and daughters of God.* The Westminster divines were almost all ministering where they would offer counseling. The human condition doesn't change. Those pastors needed to comfort the flock of Christ even as we need to today.

Dr. Joel Beeke discovered more than 1,200 pages of writing on the doctrine of adoption from the age of the Puritans in seventeenth-century England, Wales, Ireland and Scotland, and the Netherlands.[27] Yet little has been reproduced. Perhaps we are not doing as good a job as the Puritans in feeding our flock on the word of the Lord concerning God's doctrine of adoption.

Reflections from Contemporary Pastor-Scholars

Dr. John Piper, the pastor of preaching and vision at the Bethlehem Baptist Church in Minneapolis, Minnesota, included in a sermon about adoption the story of their child born to them through adoption. He made the following bold affirmation of faith:

> Adoption is one of the most profound realities in the universe. I say "universe" and not "world" because adoption goes beyond the world. It is greater than the world, and it is before the world in the plan of God, and it will outlast the world, as we know it. Indeed it is greater than the "universe" and is rooted in God's own nature.[28]

To learn everything we need to know about adoption through God's grace we could simply get a copy of the 1973 classic book *Knowing God* by the eminent Anglican theologian, J. I. Packer, and read his chapter, "Sons of God." There may be no greater summary of the doctrine of adoption than the following glorious passage by Packer:

> Adoption is the highest privilege that the gospel offers: higher even than justification. . . . That justification—by

which we mean God's forgiveness of the past together with his acceptance for the future—is the primary and fundamental blessing of the gospel is not in question. Justification is the primary blessing, because it meets our primary spiritual need. We all stand by nature under God's judgment; his law condemns us; guilt gnaws at us, making us restless, miserable and in our lucid moments afraid; we have no peace in ourselves because we have no peace with our Maker. So we need the forgiveness of our sins, and assurance of a restored relationship with God, more than we need anything else in the world; and this the gospel offers before it offers us anything else. . . . But this is not to say that justification is the highest blessing of the gospel. Adoption is higher, because of the richer relationship with God that it involves. . . . Adoption is a family idea, conceived in terms of love, and viewing God as father. In adoption, God takes us into his family and fellowship and he establishes us as his children and heirs. Closeness, affection and generosity are at the heart of the relationship. To be right with God the judge is a great thing, but to be loved and cared for by God the Father is greater.[29]

FOUR FINAL THOUGHTS ON THE DOCTRINE OF ADOPTION

1. The doctrine of adoption attributes the initiative for the relationship between God and fallen humanity to God.

I would again cite just two of our examples.

But to all who did receive him, who believed in his name, he gave the right to become children of God,

who were born, not of blood nor of the will of the flesh
nor of the will of man, but of God. (John 1:12–13)

He predestined us for adoption as sons through Jesus
Christ, according to the purpose of his will. (Eph. 1:5)

We are as passive in adoption as a little baby is when
I hold that child over the baptismal font. Indeed, my systematic theology professor, Dr. Robert L. Reymond, used
to tell us seminarians that the most beautiful picture of
God's election, with all of its accompanying graces, is seen
in a sleeping infant receiving the sacrament of baptism.[30]
In baptism, the child is completely passive. What has happened to that child being born (whether through adoption or
not) into a Christian family, receiving all of the blessings,
benefits, covenant promises, and spiritual advantages is
wholly outside of her control. In fact, she is sleeping through
it all. So it is with adoption.

It is out of deep, unfathomable oceans of divine grace
that you were chosen by God and for His holy and unsearchable purposes to His own glory. You cannot fathom the depth
of that love or conceive of the purposes in His secret counsel.[31] All you know is what He has revealed to you in His
inerrant and infallible Word: when you repented and believed
in Jesus Christ as the living Lord and only Savior of sinners, you were adopted as the Father's son or daughter. This
is a once and for all act of almighty God, not an ongoing
identity. Again, as Russell Moore puts it, "adoption is a past
tense verb," and that is as true in spiritual adoption as it is
in family adoption on earth; you were adopted, you are a son
or a daughter of the Father, now and forever.[32] In fact, you
may be reading this and have never fully understood the
doctrine. Yet if you have repented of your sins of trusting in

anyone or anything other than the Redeemer, the crucified, resurrected, ascended, and returning Christ, then you have been adopted by Him into His family. This is God's work and yours. The doctrine of adoption, like all doctrines recovered and reclaimed by the reformers (which we called the doctrines of the Reformed faith), humbles mankind. It destroys the works-righteousness of mankind in his attempted relationship with God and exalts the redemptive work of God in Christ that restores the fallen creature to his Creator.

2. The doctrine of adoption acknowledges that we are part of a greater family.

> One body, and one Spirit, even as ye are called in one hope of your calling. (Eph. 4:4 KJV)

Because all holy doctrine is connected, adoption connects us to the one, holy, catholic (pure, true global, timeless body of Christ) church. No longer can we think of ourselves in a private Christianity or ever believe again that our faith is just "a personal matter." Rather, we are adopted into a true, organic family of God with all rights as fellow heirs with Christ. The terms "brothers," "sisters," "fathers," and "mothers" in the faith are not just cute colloquial ways of addressing each other in the closing line of our letters. They are not some "clubby" insider terms of a closed society. Such filial terms are emotionally rich, unassailably real, and overflowing with deep theological, biblical, and even "blood-redeemed" meaning. They acknowledge our purchase from sin and our adoption in one common holy family. The doctrine of adoption means that we, the Father's children, have *life together*.[33]
It is critical, therefore, to see in this passage that there is one body of Christ, not two or three, or more. There is one.

There is one Spirit who baptizes us all into that body. There is one hope of our calling, and that is the hope to eternal life through Jesus Christ our Lord.[34]

The doctrine of adoption tells us that we are part of a family. We are not only part of a visible family, but also an invisible family that includes those family members in Christ who have gone before us. The church militant—those of us still moving on in Christ on earth—and the church triumphant—those who have gone from this life into the very presence of Christ—are all one family as well. We are truly a "communion of saints."[35]

As A. A. Hodge, of old Princeton, wrote, "Adoption presents the new creature in his new relations—his new relations entered upon with a congenial heart, and his new life developing in a congenial home, and surrounded with those relations which foster its growth and crown it with blessedness."[36] This is the church,[37] your family, and your new forever home.

3. The doctrine of adoption brings a special ministry of the Holy Spirit, which Scripture calls the "Spirit of adoption."

> For you did not receive the spirit of slavery to fall back into fear, but you have received the Spirit of adoption as sons, by whom we cry, "Abba Father!" (Rom. 8:15)

The revealed work of the Holy Spirit in our adoption as the Father's sons and daughters is the consequence of the judicial act of adoption and not the cause.[38] This work of the Spirit seals the relationship of parent with child, of your Father God with you. The third person of the Trinity comes upon you—the repentant one who trusts wholly in Jesus Christ—and completes a work of holy transformation. This makes you His true child who can never be thought of as a "cosmic orphan" any longer.[39] Again, by the Spirit's initiative, the Spirit is a gift who seals you—the redeemed one—to the Father forever. "And because you are sons, God *has sent* the Spirit of his Son into our hearts, crying, 'Abba Father!' " (Gal. 4:6).

I like the way John Murray described this unique activity of the Holy Spirit in the sequence of redemption revealed in the Bible.

> The act of adoption is necessary to the possession of the prerogative of sons; the Spirit of adoption to the cultivation of these prerogatives and the fulfillment of the correlative obligations. It is the Spirit of adoption who produces the highest confidence that it is given to men to exercise in relation to God. The people of God thereby recognize not only Christ as their Redeemer and Saviour, high priest and advocate at God's right hand, not only the Holy Spirit as their sanctifier and advocate, not only the Father as the one who has called them into the fellowship of his Son but also as the one who has instated them in his family, and they enter into the holiest in the assurance that he, the God and Father of the Lord Jesus Christ, will own them and bless them as his own children.[40]

4. The holy doctrine of adoption attests to the biblical fact that there are two classes of mankind: those who have been adopted and those who have not.

All of God's children were adopted into His family. The world is filled with those who are His by adoption into His family and those who are not. There can be no in-between place. You are a child of God through faith in Christ or you are not a child of God.

The doctrine of adoption clearly teaches that we cannot be Christians when we are born. God has no naturally born children. Called children of wrath, we were conceived in sin, born in sin, and bear the marks of rebellion. We may help mankind but still be at enmity with God. We must be born again, as our Lord taught Nicodemus in the third chapter of John's gospel, in order to be a child of God. God chooses His children, for the "wind blows where it wishes" (John 3:8). New birth is not of man, but of God. Yet, graciously, mercifully, the Bible allows us to view regeneration, justification, and adoption through the lens that best fits our earthly eyes when it says we are given the right to become children of God if we come to Him. Jesus calls us to come to Him and He will receive us. He will never turn away. That is the way things look this side of heaven. But the doctrine of adoption shows us that behind the scenes it was really the Lord who chose us to be His own before the foundation of the world. Thank God.

Are you a child of His? Do you think that perhaps being born into a Christian family is enough? It is not. As a child within a Christian family, you are given unique privileges for which you are responsible. Yet you too must be born again by taking advantage of those blessed covenantal privileges and claiming your heritage as God's child. This comes through repentance and faith in the resurrected and living Christ. The Holy Spirit will wash you from the inside out and confirm the promises made over you, perhaps made when you were baptized as an infant. God will seal you as His own child. He will never let go of anyone who comes into His hands.

Today, even as you read this, receive Christ. Today, renew your commitment to Him and come home to Him. If you have wandered far, it is time for you to see your Father waiting for you. There is a great banquet of abundant life and love and family awaiting your return. I know. I was one who came and received. This orphan was adopted. I was given a name. I was given hope. I was given family. What God did in my life and in so many other lives, He will do for you. You are His child.

A *REAL* SON

Michael Reagan, the famous radio talk show host and the son of Ronald Reagan, tells an insightful story about the power and reality of adoption in his book, *Twice Adopted*.[41] Michael Reagan writes that he received a call from his son's teacher. She was worried about Cameron. The thoughtful teacher had noticed that something was troubling Cameron—to the point of tears.

"Where is he now?"
"On the front steps of the school—crying."

Michael Reagan left his work and went immediately to his son. He sat down beside Cameron and asked him what was wrong. The third-grader, heaving tears, strengthened himself enough to ask one penetrating question.

"Daddy," he said, "is Grandpa really my grandpa?"
"Of course he is," I said. "Why do you ask?"
He looked down at his shoes. "Because one of the kids told me that you're adopted. And if you're adopted, you're not really Grandpa's son. And if you're not really his son, then Grandpa's not really my grandpa."[42]

Michael Reagan felt an old pain inside his own heart. Reagan said that the words went through him "like a spear, hitting me in one of my most vulnerable places: my adoption." He went on to admit that this message had hurt him all his life. Although his father had made it clear to him that he was his son and there were no more questions about it, others were thoughtless, hurtful, and even downright mean. It always seemed that the reporters couldn't just write, "Ronald Reagan's son," but Reagan's "adopted son."

Michael Reagan had come to know better though. He had come to Christ. He had learned that no one gets into heaven without being adopted. All of us are His adopted children. As we have seen, Jesus even modeled this doctrine in His earthly life with Joseph. Michael Reagan knew that. The pain had to give way to truth, no matter how senseless or thoughtless others might be or how cruel a schoolyard bully might be to his little boy. Michael Reagan's response was powerful because it was simple and real.

> "Cameron," I said, "I was adopted into the Reagan family, and the Reagan family is my family. President Reagan is my father, and he's your Grandpa. You are the grandson of the President and part of his family just like I am." I pointed toward a man wearing a dark suit and sunglasses. "If you weren't the grandson of the President, you wouldn't have Secret Service agents around you all the time, would you?"
>
> He looked at the agent, grinned at me, "I guess not."[43]

Child of God, anytime you doubt your relationship to the Father, just look at the cross. One of the devil's greatest attacks is to do what that schoolyard bully did to Cameron

Reagan: to disturb the identity of the child of God with his unwitting agents who say thoughtless, mean, and false teachings. Remember the truth—you are His child. If you have repented and turned to Christ in faith, then you are born again. You are sealed and marked as the very child of God. If it were not so, then Christ would not have told you so. God would not have sent His Son to die on a cross to redeem you, to buy you back, to rescue you from a life of sin and shame and eternal separation from Him. If you are not God's real child, then the work of Christ means nothing. But look at the cross. Would the cross be there if you were not His?

The doctrine of adoption is essential to the believer's assurance. You are saved without having to know all of the details. But you will never be fully happy until you know that you know that you know that you are His child. God is your Father. He will never leave you or forsake you the way some earthly fathers may. He will lavish His love upon you. With His Son Jesus Christ you are His heir of all things. No, you are not the one and only Son, nor will you ever be the Son of God the way Jesus Christ is. But you are His son, His daughter, forever and ever because He gave you to Jesus before the world began.[44] Jesus came to pay the price of bringing you into God's family. He was raised again from the dead, which verified His identity as the unique Son of the Father. The full testimony of Scripture comes to you today, with the power of the Holy Spirit, to draw you to see His love for you.

If you know this doctrine, then you are blessed. If you do not, or if you are in a situation like Cameron, where people or events have conspired to take your family joy from you, maybe because of your sin or the sin of another, just remember the cross. You are His child. He claimed you as His own. Even death cannot separate you from Him.

> Who shall separate us from the love of Christ? Shall tribulation, or distress, or persecution, or famine, or nakedness, or danger, or sword? As it is written, "For your sake we are being killed all the day long; we are regarded as sheep to be slaughtered." No, in all these things we are more than conquerors through him who loved us. For I am sure that neither death nor life, nor angels nor rulers, nor things present nor things to come, nor powers, nor height nor depth, nor anything else in all creation, will be able to separate us from the love of God in Christ Jesus our Lord. (Rom. 8:35–39)

Indeed, it is only a portal through which you will now move to be welcomed home by your Father.[45]

Like Michael Reagan, we can be set free as we learn and glory in the truth of our adoption as true sons and true daughters: "God is my Father, and I am His child. I'm finally home."[46] This is the identity and the eternal destination for God's *real* sons and daughters. This, then, *is* the doctrine of adoption.

To God our Father be all glory and honor, now and forevermore.

REFERENCES

"Adoption." Monergism. http://www.monergism.com/directory/link _category/Adoption/ [accessed December 1, 2010].

Badie, Katie. "The Prayer of Humble Access." *The Churchman*. http:// www.churchsociety.org/churchman/documents/Cman_120_2 _Badie.pdf [accessed December 29, 2010].

Bannerman, James. *The Church of Christ: A Treatise on the Nature, Powers, Ordinances, Discipline, and Government of the Christian Church*. 2 vols. [London]: Banner of Truth Trust, 1960.

Beeke, Joel R. *Heirs with Christ: The Puritans on Adoption*. Grand Rapids, MI: Reformation Heritage Books, 2008.

Bonar, Andrew Alexander. *The Life and Remains, Letters, Lectures, and Poems of the Rev. Robert Murray M'Cheyne*. New York: Robert Carter, 1847.

Bonhoeffer, Dietrich. *Life Together*. 1st Harper & Row pbk. ed. New York: Harper & Row, 1954.

Calvin, John. *Calvin's Bible Commentaries: Isaiah, Part IV*. Translated by John King: Forgotten Books. Reprint, 2007.

Church of England. *The Book of Common Prayer and Administration of the Sacraments and Other Rites and Ceremonies of the Church According to the Use of the Church of England: Together with the Psalter, or Psalms of David, Pointed as They Are to Be Sung or Said in Churches*. London: Printed by John Bill and Christopher Barker, 1662.

Clowney, Edmund P. *The Church*. Contours of Christian Theology. Downers Grove, IL: InterVarsity Press, 1995.

Ferguson, Sinclair B. *Children of the Living God*. Colorado Springs, CO: NavPress, 1987.

Hodge, Archibald Alexander. *The Confession of Faith: A Handbook of Christian Doctrine Expounding the Westminster Confession*. London: Banner of Truth Trust, 1964.

Horner, Susan E., and Kelly Fordyce Martindale. *Loved by Choice: True Stories That Celebrate Adoption*. Grand Rapids, MI: Fleming H. Revell, 2002.

Johnston, Mark G. *Child of a King*. Focus on Faith. Fearn: Christian Focus, 1997.

Milton, Michael A. *What Is the Doctrine of the Perseverance of the Saints?* Basics of the Reformed Faith. Phillipsburg, NJ: P&R Publishing, 2009.

Milton, Michael Anthony. *Through the Open Door*. Compact Disc Recording. Matthews, NC: Bethesda Words and Music, 2011.

Moore, Russell. *Adopted for Life: The Priority of Adoption for Christian Families and Churches*. Wheaton, IL: Crossway Books, 2009.

Murray, John. "Adoption." *Reformationfiles.com* (2010). http://www.reformationfiles.com/files/displaytext.php?file=murray_adoption.html [accessed December 29, 2010].

Murray, John. *Redemption, Accomplished and Applied*. Grand Rapids: W. B. Eerdmans, 1955.

New Reformation Study Bible: English Standard Version. 1st ed. Phillipsburg, NJ: P&R Publishing, 2005.

Packer, J. I. *Knowing God*. 20th anniversary ed. Downers Grove, IL: InterVarsity Press, 1993.

Peterson, Robert A. *Adopted by God: From Wayward Sinners to Cherished Children*. Phillipsburg, NJ: P&R Publishing, 2001.

Piper, John. "Predestined to Adoption to the Praise of His Glory: Reflections on Being Adopted by God and Adopting Children." *A Sermon before Bethlehem Baptist Church* (June 20, 2004). http://www.desiringgod.org/resource-library/resources/predestined-for-adoption-to-the-praise-of-his-glory.

Ray, Charles. "Prayer of Humble Access." *Anglicans in the Wilderness*. http://anglo-reformed.org/prayer-of-humble-access [accessed December 29, 2010].

Reagan, Michael, and Jim Denney. *Twice Adopted*. Nashville: Broadman & Holman, 2004.

Reymond, Robert L. *A New Systematic Theology of the Christian Faith*. Nashville: T. Nelson, 1998.

Rosner, Brian S., and T. Desmond Alexander. *New Dictionary of Biblical Theology IVP Reference Collection*. Leicester: InterVarsity Press, 2000.

Ryken, Philip Graham. *The Communion of Saints: Living in Fellowship with the People of God*. Phillipsburg, NJ: P&R Publishing, 2001.

Spurgeon, Charles Haddon. "Lydia, the First European Convert." *The Spurgeon Archive*, Sermon no. 2222 (September 20th, 1891). http://www.spurgeon.org/sermons/2222.htm [accessed December 29, 2010].

Taylor, Justin. "From Adopted to Adopting." *Boundless Webzine: A Website of Focus on the Family* (2007). http://www.boundless.org/2005/articles/a0001609.cfm [accessed November 29, 2010].

Watson, Thomas. *A Body of Divinity, Contained in Sermons Upon the Westminster Assembly's Catechism*. Revised ed.: Banner of Truth Trust, 1965.

The Westminster Shorter Catechism: With Scripture Proofs. Edinburgh: Banner of Truth Trust, 2008.

NOTES

1 *The Westminster Shorter Catechism: With Scripture Proofs* (Edinburgh: Banner of Truth Trust, 2008).

2 John Murray, *Redemption, Accomplished and Applied* (Grand Rapids: W. B. Eerdmans, 1955), 132.

3 "Grace to you and peace from God our Father and the Lord Jesus Christ, who gave himself for our sins to deliver us from the present evil age, according to the will of our God and Father" (Gal. 1:3–4).

4 Joel R. Beeke, *Heirs with Christ: The Puritans on Adoption* (Grand Rapids, MI: Reformation Heritage Books, 2008), xi.

5 "But to all who did receive him, who believed in his name, he gave the right to become children of God, who were born, not of blood nor of the will of the flesh nor of the will of man, but of God" (John 1:12–13).

6 See " 'Are They Brothers?' What Some Rude Questions about Adoption Taught Me about the Gospel of Christ" by Russell D. Moore, *Adopted for Life: The Priority of Adoption for Christian Families & Churches* (Wheaton, IL: Crossway Books, 2009).

7 Justin Taylor, "From Adopted to Adopting," *Boundless Webzine: A Website of Focus on the Family* (2007), http://www.boundless.org/2005/articles/a0001609.cfm (accessed November 29, 2010).

8 R. E. Ciampa, "Adoption," in Brian S. Rosner and T. Desmond Alexander, *New Dictionary of Biblical Theology*, IVP Reference Collection (Leicester: Inter-Varsity Press, 2000), 376.

9 The best summary and application of this biblical truth is found in *The Book of Common Prayer's* "A Table of Kindred and Affinity." See Church of England, *The Book of Common Prayer and Administration of the Sacraments and Other Rites and Ceremonies of the Church According to the Use of the Church of England: Together with the Psalter, or Psalms of David, Pointed as They Are to Be Sung or Said in Churches* (London: Printed by John Bill and Christopher Barker, 1662). This may also

be found online at http://justus.anglican.org/resources/bcp/1662/Kindred1949.htm.

10 Misconceptions about children born to families through adoption include the myth of a perpetually and deeply wounded and damaged person forever in search of wholeness. Such hypotheses were printed in abundance in the 1960s and 1970s, and are, in this pastor's estimation, regrettably understandable apologetics for the abortion rights movement. For a more realistic evaluation of adoption from a Christian perspective read Susan E. Horner and Kelly Fordyce Martindale, *Loved by Choice: True Stories That Celebrate Adoption* (Grand Rapids, MI: Fleming H. Revell, 2002). This book assaults the ideology or philosophy of human beings finding identity in self rather than God.

11 Thomas Watson, *A Body of Divinity, Contained in Sermons Upon the Westminster Assembly's Catechism*, rev. ed. (Banner of Truth Trust, 1965). I quote from "Adoption," Monergism, http://www.monergism.com/directory/link_category/Adoption/ (accessed December 1, 2010).

12 If you want deeper reading on the subject, I highly recommend the following: Sinclair B. Ferguson, *Children of the Living God* (Colorado Springs, CO: NavPress, 1987); Joel R. Beeke, *Heirs with Christ: The Puritans on Adoption* (Grand Rapids, MI: Reformation Heritage Books, 2008); Mark G. Johnston, *Child of a King*, Focus on Faith (Fearn: Christian Focus, 1997); Robert A. Peterson, *Adopted by God: From Wayward Sinners to Cherished Children* (Phillipsburg, NJ: P&R, 2001).

13 Murray identified Exodus 4:22, 23; Deuteronomy 14:1, 2; cf. 1:31; Deuteronomy 32:5, 6, 20; Isaiah 43:6; cf. Isaiah 1:2; Isaiah 63:16; Hosea 11:1; Malachi 1:6; Malachi 2:10; and he added Romans 9:4 (in which Paul speaks of adoption as belonging to the old covenant people of God). I have added the narratives of Rahab and Ruth for selected examples in the paragraphs that follow, not as exhaustive ones. I would also add the Psalms of Ascent, Psalms 120-135, as psalms in which the doctrine of adoption is taught. As the people went up each year to festivals at Jerusalem, God reminded them through these psalms that they were His children. The histories, the epic sweep of His covenant love to Israel, are recalled in these psalms. Psalm 135:4, the final Psalm of Ascent, culminates, in

a way, with a beautiful validation of Israel's adoption into God's family: "For the LORD has chosen Jacob for himself, Israel as His own possession."

14 The earthly line of Jesus is identified through His earthly father Joseph. In this way Christ also embodies the doctrine of adoption in His own lineage.

15 "And because he loved your fathers and chose their offspring after them and brought you out of Egypt with his own presence, by his great power" (Deut. 4:37); "It was not because you were more in number than any other people that the LORD set his love on you and chose you, for you were the fewest of all peoples" (Deut. 7:7); "Do not say in your heart, after the LORD your God has thrust them out before you, 'It is because of my righteousness that the LORD has brought me in to possess this land,' whereas it is because of the wickedness of these nations that the LORD is driving them out before you" (Deut. 9:4); "Yet the LORD set his heart in love on your fathers and chose their offspring after them, you above all peoples, as you are this day" (Deut. 10:15).

16 John Calvin, *Calvin's Bible Commentaries: Isaiah*, Part IV, trans. John King (Forgotten Books; reprint, 2007), 324.

17 Ibid.

18 "Looking to Jesus the author and finisher of our faith; who for the joy that was set before him endured the cross, despising the shame, and is set down at the right hand of the throne of God" (Heb. 12:2 KJV).

19 Matthew 8:5–13 and Luke 7:1–9.

20 This faithful response of the Roman soldier is also found in Luke 7:8. As for the liturgical note, this response "is a [Thomas] Cranmer legacy, perhaps the first of Cranmer's own compositions to feature in the Anglican liturgy" which went through a series of changes before landing for centuries in the *Book of Common Prayer* based on the 1662 version. It appears today in the 1928 *American Book of Common Prayer* and is said between the Words of Institution and the Distribution of the Elements. I go into this detail at this point to show how the simple response of an otherwise alien to God and His people revealed his faith that led him to justification and adoption as a son of God. That we use the words of a Roman soldier to approach the Table of the Lord in Holy Communion is a testimony to the grace of God to sinners and to how, having adopted

us into His family, we are truly His family. For more on this see Katie Badie, "The Prayer of Humble Access," The Churchman, http://www .churchsociety.org/churchman/documents/Cman_120_2_Badie .pdf (accessed December 29, 2010); Charles Ray, "Prayer of Humble Access," Anglicans in the Wilderness, http://anglo-reformed.org /prayer-of-humble-access (accessed December 29, 2010).

21 Matthew 8:10; Luke 7:9.

22 "So, setting sail from Troas, we made a direct voyage to Samothrace, and the following day to Neapolis, and from there to Philippi, which is a leading city of the district of Macedonia and a Roman colony. We remained in this city some days. And on the Sabbath day we went outside the gate to the riverside, where we supposed there was a place of prayer, and we sat down and spoke to the women who had come together. One who heard us was a woman named Lydia, from the city of Thyatira, a seller of purple goods, who was a worshiper of God. The Lord opened her heart to pay attention to what was said by Paul. And after she was baptized, and her household as well, she urged us, saying, 'If you have judged me to be faithful to the Lord, come to my house and stay.' And she prevailed upon us" (Acts 16:11-15).

23 Charles Haddon Spurgeon, "Lydia, the First European Convert," The Spurgeon Archive, Sermon no. 2222 (September 20th, 1891), http:// www.spurgeon.org/sermons/2222.htm (accessed December 29, 2010).

24 The heresy of "adoptionism," which arose in the second century, primarily popularized by one Theodotus of Byzantium (late 2nd century) in his writings, denied the two natures of Christ—God and Man—and claimed that Jesus was a mere man, then "adopted" by God the Father upon His baptism, assuming the nature of divinity only after the resurrection. This confusing false teaching, also called Dynamic Monarchianism, was condemned by Pope Victor I (AD 190-198).

See the following biblical teachings: "For in him the whole fullness of deity dwells bodily" (Col. 2:9). "He is the radiance of the glory of God and the exact imprint of his nature, and he upholds the universe by the word of his power. After making purification for sins, he sat down at the right hand of the Majesty on high" (Heb. 1:3). "And the Word was made flesh, and dwelt among us, (and we beheld his glory, the glory as of the only begotten of the Father,) full of grace and truth" (John 1:14 KJV). Therefore one must be careful and quite clear in speaking about

Jesus and His adoption. He was the God-Man, the only begotten of the Father, and adopted in His earthly life as the son of Joseph.

25 Randall J. Pederson, ed., *George Whitefield Daily Readings* (Geanies House, Fearn, Tain, Ross-shire, Scotland, UK: Christian Heritage imprint by Christian Focus Publications, 2010), January 10th reading.

26 Beeke, 9,10.

27 See Beeke, 13.

28 John Piper, "Predestined to Adoption to the Praise of His Glory: Reflections on Being Adopted by God and Adopting Children," A Sermon before Bethlehem Baptist Church (June 20, 2004), http://www.desiringgod.org/resource-library/resources /predestined-for-adoption-to-the-praise-of-his-glory.

29 J. I. Packer, *Knowing God*, 20th anniversary ed. (Downers Grove, IL: InterVarsity Press, 1993).

30 See Robert L. Reymond, *A New Systematic Theology of the Christian Faith* (Nashville: T. Nelson, 1998).

31 I paraphrase the impressive words of Robert Murray M'Cheyne who wrote, "Unfathomable oceans of grace are in Christ for you. Dive and dive again, you will never come to the bottom of these depths. How many millions of dazzling pearls and gems are at this moment hid in the deep recesses of the ocean caves! But there are unsearchable riches in Christ. Seek more of them. The Lord will enrich you with them." See Andrew Alexander Bonar, *The Life and Remains, Letters, Lectures, and Poems of the Rev. Robert Murray M'Cheyne* (New York: Robert Carter, 1847), 205.

32 I wrote a song for my wife called "Now and Forever," which I sang to her at our wedding June 8, 1985, and which I recorded for her on the album *Through the Open Door*, in January 2011. The song is a love song that reflects the love of Christ for His own children. Just as the song says, you are His "Now and forevermore." God will not adopt you into His family, give you His Spirit, and then somehow take it away because you have made a mistake. See Michael Anthony Milton, *Through the Open Door* (Matthews, NC: Bethesda Words and Music), Compact Disc Recording, released January 31, 2011.

33 See Dietrich Bonhoeffer, *Life Together*, 1st Harper & Row pbk. ed. (New York: Harper & Row, 1954).

34 See also Edmund P. Clowney, *The Church*, Contours of Christian Theology (Downers Grove, IL: InterVarsity Press, 1995).

35 See Philip Graham Ryken, *The Communion of Saints: Living in Fellowship with the People of God* (Phillipsburg, NJ: P&R Publishing, 2001).

36 Archibald Alexander Hodge, *The Confession of Faith: A Handbook of Christian Doctrine Expounding the Westminster Confession* (London: Banner of Truth Trust, 1964), 192.

37 See James Bannerman, *The Church of Christ: A Treatise on the Nature, Powers, Ordinances, Discipline, and Government of the Christian Church*, 2 vols. ([London]: Banner of Truth Trust, 1960).

38 Again, we must be careful to differentiate between the work of regeneration and justification. The Holy Spirit is certainly the one who draws us to Christ and works grace within us, whereby we are led to call on God, repent, and believe, resulting in our justification before a holy God. The result of the judicial act of adoption into God's family through Christ brings about a change in our inner mind and spirit, leading us to respond to this gracious act and cry out in our heart with joy and new life.

39 While the truths revealed in Scripture may be isolated for study and to discern the progress and sequence of redemption in our lives by Christ, all doctrine is beautifully woven together. Thus there is a lovely relationship between the perseverance of the saints and the doctrine of adoption that brings about assurance of faith in the believer. See Michael A. Milton, *What Is the Doctrine of the Perseverance of the Saints?* (Phillipsburg, NJ: P&R Publishing, 2009).

40 See the article by John Murray, "Adoption," Reformationfiles .com (2010), http://www.reformationfiles.com/files/displaytext .php?file=murray_adoption.html (accessed December 29, 2010).

41 Michael Reagan and Jim Denney, *Twice Adopted* (Nashville: Broadman & Holman, 2004).

42 Ibid., 283.

43 Ibid., 284.

44 "My sheep hear my voice, and I know them, and they follow me. I give them eternal life, and they will never perish, and no one will snatch them out of my hand. My Father, who has given them to me, is greater than all, and no one is able to snatch them out of the Father's hand" (John 10:27–29).

45 "Precious in the sight of the LORD is the death of his saints" (Ps. 116:15).

46 Reagan, 318.

ALSO BY MIKE MILTON

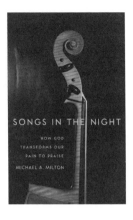

Price: $14.99
To order, visit www.prpbooks.com
Or call 1(800) 631-0094

Turn your weakest, most discouraging moments . . . into your best,
most uplifting moments.

These pastoral messages and personal illustrations show how the
brokenhearted Christian can locate the God of all comfort in the
center of their pain, and can even learn how the gospel transforms
our private pain into personal praise.

"Mike's book won me immediately. You can tell that Mike has been
a pastor and someone who has suffered personally. Pastors and
sufferers can never be content with a theoretical answer to suffering.
You must wisely develop a practical theology of suffering. *Songs in
the Night* is just that."

—**Tim Lane,** President, The Christian Counseling
and Educational Foundation

MORE FROM P&R PUBLISHING

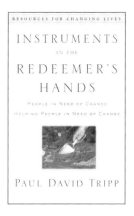

Price: $16.99
To order, visit www.prpbooks.com
Or call 1(800) 631-0094

Paul Tripp helps us discover where change is needed in our own lives and the lives of others. Following the example of Jesus, Tripp reveals how to get to know people, and how to lovingly speak truth to them.

"Helps us help others (and ourselves) by giving grace-centered hope that we can indeed change, and by showing us the biblical way to make change happen."

—**Skip Ryan**

"Tripp unites a loving heart with a mind trained to the Scriptures. This book is a great companion for pastors and counselors. It will guide anyone who wants to give real help to others, the saving help that is found in Christ's redeeming work."

—**Richard D. Phillips**

MORE FROM P&R PUBLISHING

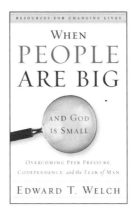

Price: $15.99
To order, visit www.prpbooks.com
Or call 1(800) 631-0094

"Need people less. Love people more. That's the author's challenge.
. . . He's talking about a tendency to hold other people in awe, to be
controlled and mastered by them, to depend on them for what God
alone can give. . . . [Welch] proposes an antidote: the fear of God."

—*Dallas Morning News*

"Biblical and practical. . . . Opens our eyes and directs us back to
God and his Word to overcome the fear of man."

—*The Baptist Bulletin*

"Much needed in our own day. . . . Here is a volume that church librar-
ies and book tables ought to have. Its theme is contemporary. Its
answer is thoroughly biblical."

—*The Presbyterian Witness*